My Little Handbook of Feelings

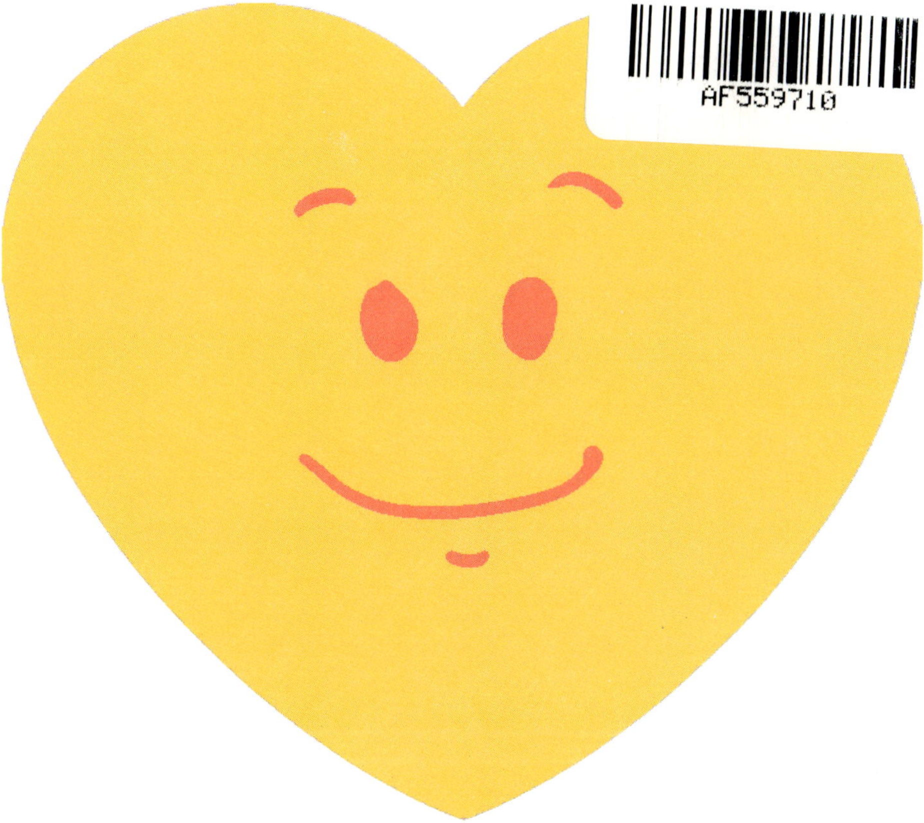

ARTIKA AURORA BAKSHI

Illustrated by Priyankar Gupta

THE BROWSER

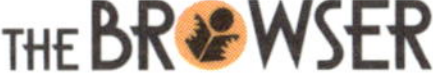

Title: My Little Handbook of Feelings
Author: Artika Aurora Bakshi

ISBN: 978-93-92210-56-3

Published by:
JGS Enterprises Pvt Ltd
Imprint: The Browser

Publisher's Address:
SCO 14-15, FF, Sector 8-C, Chandigarh 160 009
Website: thebrowser.org
Email: service@thebrowser.org

Book design by Bhavi Mehta

Printed in India

Publishers & Booksellers

This handbook belongs to

For Hashmat and Himmat,
my joy and my strength!

"There are days when I feel lots of things, and I don't know what to do," said Joey to Miss Gil.

The children had come to school after their summer holidays. Miss Gil made them sit in a circle. She could see that some of the children were not smiling.

"We all have hearts, and our hearts feel a lot of things. Let's start with Joey. What is your heart feeling right now, Joey?" asked Miss Gil.

GEOMETRIC SHAPES
School timetable
1 2 3 4 5 6 7 8 9
Mon
Tue
Wed
Thu
Fri

"My heart doesn't want to smile because Anya is not smiling," said Joey.

Anya looked at Miss Gil and said, "I am missing my Mummy today."

"Anya's heart is sad because she is away from her Mummy today," said Miss Gil, giving Anya a hug. "Anya, you can go home to Mummy later. We can all make your heart feel better," she said. "What makes your hearts sad?" she asked the class.

ACTIVITY 1

Things that make little hearts SAD

1. Losing something special

2. ....

....

3. ....

....

4. ....

....

5. ....

....

"When someone is sad, ask them why, and then do something to make them feel better," explained Miss Gil.

Anya smiled.

Joey smiled too.

"There are many things that we can do to make our hearts happy," said Miss Gil.

Activity 2

Things that make sad hearts HAPPY

1. A hug from someone special

2. ....

....

3. ....

....

4. ....

....

5. ....

....

"Now tell me about the other things you feel," continued Miss Gil, looking at all the children in her class. "I feel happy when Himmat sits next to me," said Nadia, with a beaming smile.

"That is because I am happy," laughed Himmat.

"What makes you happy, Himmat?" asked Miss Gil.

"Rainbows," he beamed.

ACTIVITY 3

Draw a happy picture with the things that make little hearts happy

"What else do you feel?" asked Miss Gil, looking at all the children.

"Sometimes when Pia pushes me, I want to squeeze my eyes shut, and stamp my feet," said Lee, with a frown. "She makes me angry."

The teacher listened as Lee continued, "Sometimes Pia and I fight."

"Our hearts feel angry too. But then, we have to find out what makes our hearts angry," explained Miss Gil.

"I get angry when he takes my things without asking me," said Pia.

"When things make you angry, you should sit down and count to 10," said Miss Gil.

"Sometimes when we sit down, our anger goes away, and then we do not stamp our feet or shout."

"I know that we should say sorry when we get angry," said Avi.

"Very good," said Miss Gil, patting Avi's head. "And Lee, please do not take anything without asking."

ACTIVITY 4

Colour SORRY. Draw an ANGRY face and a HAPPY face.

SORRY

"There are many things that can make hearts angry," said Miss Gil.

When we DO NOT want to do something.

When someone SHOUTS at us.

When we DO NOT get what we want.

When our friends DO NOT play with us.

"When I am angry, a hug from my Mummy makes me feel better," chipped in Pia.

"No one can stay angry for a long time. By being nice when someone is angry, you can make their heart feel better," said Miss Gil.

"We can also tickle them and make them laugh," grinned Himmat.

"We are all different, but our feelings are the same. Sometimes, our hearts are happy, and sometimes they feel sad," explained Miss Gil.

Everyone was listening to the teacher. They loved her. Just then, Zack got up to get the water bottle. The bottle slipped from his hands. It looked as if he was ready to cry.

Miss Gil went up to him and gave him a hug.

"Don't worry. It was an accident," she said.

"That was clumsy," pointed Sue.

"You might feel embarrassed, but that is okay. Mistakes happen," said Miss Gil.

"Do you remember how you feel when you spill something all over your clothes?"

"Or when we slip while running?" added Sue.

"I always say sorry when I spill something," said Himmat.

"That is good," smiled Miss Gil, clapping her hands.

"I think Zack got scared," said Zo.

"I thought everyone would get angry with me," replied Zack.

"There are times when you are scared, but there is nothing to be scared of," observed Miss Gil.

"There are some things that scare me," said Zo.

"Would you like to tell us about the things that scare you?" asked Miss Gil.

5 Write down the things that SCARE you

1. Loud Noises

2. ....

3. ....

4. ....

We all
FEEL
differently.
SPEAK
about your
FEELINGS.
Mommy,
Daddy,
our teachers
and friends are
always there
to LOVE us.
It is
ALRIGHT.
DO NOT make
fun of anyone's
FEELINGS.

The children got together and clapped for their teacher.

The bell rang, and it was time to go home.
"Go home, happy hearts," said Miss Gil as she made them line up and leave the classroom.

ACTIVITY 6

What are they FEELING?

ANGRY

....

....

SAD

EXCITED

....

LOVED

....

....

SCARED

MY DAY IN PICTURES

MY DAY TODAY

MY DAY IN PICTURES

MY DAY TODAY

MY DAY IN PICTURES

MY DAY TODAY

MY DAY IN PICTURES

ACKNOWLEDGEMENTS

This book, like my others, comes straight from the heart. One of the most beautiful gift you can give a child is the ability to feel. In my endeavour to share this gift, here's another one in *"My Little Handbook"* series.

Himmat, Hashmat, Karen, & Maninder, thanks again for being my sounding boards, and for your feedback. Mom and Papa, thanks for always believing in all that I do.

A special thanks to Bhavi Mehta and Priyankar Gupta, who have been with me on my writing journey from the start.

Deep, Pankaj, and Mehakdeep, thanks for taking on this project.

And a special thanks to my little grandniece Pia, with whom I enjoyed talking about hearts and feelings while I had relocated to India for a brief period.

ABOUT THE AUTHOR

An avid reader, book critic, passionate writer, but most importantly, a mother, Artika Aurora Bakshi lives in a world of words. Her *My Little Sikh Handbook* series has been well-received. This is her fifth children's book.

You can find Artika on Instagram as @soul_nightingale_artika and on Facebook as Soul Nightingale by Artika Aurora Bakshi.